Little People, BIG DREAMS™
BOB DYLAN

Written by
Maria Isabel Sánchez Vegara

Illustrated by
Conrad Roset

Frances Lincoln
Children's Books

Growing up in Hibbing, Minnesota, wasn't very exciting for little Robert, the eldest son of the Zimmermans. He liked to listen to music on the radio and imagine he was somewhere else...

Inspired by his rock idols, Robert taught himself the guitar, the harmonica, and a strange instrument called the autoharp, which he played to an audience that was easily pleased.

At school, Robert would rather be invisible than draw attention to himself. When he took part in a talent show, the teacher turned his microphone off. Robert sounded like a dog whose leg was caught in barbed wire!

That didn't stop him. He experimented with rock, blues, and country music. At college, he found his rhythm playing old folk songs. The simple tunes were written by ordinary people, who told stories about everyday life.

Robert soon started composing his own songs. He had a real talent for writing rhymes and making words fit to a beat. The songs were poetic yet powerful, and he wrote them under his new name: Bob Dylan.

One year later, Bob dropped out of college and moved to New York. There, he was a nobody. But he had his guitar, his harmonica, and another useful instrument: a hat. He was determined to use it, passing it around in bars where he played.

One day, a guy from a record company came to one of his gigs. He was impressed by Bob's raw force and fresh lyrics, and offered him his first music contract. Times were changing, and Bob's life was about to change, too.

Bob's music spoke about things that mattered: civil rights, war, and religion. Without trying, he became the voice of a generation eager to change the world, putting down in words what millions of people felt.

His songs became anthems sung by the most amazing artists of all times, reaching millions of people. Many of them had not heard his voice or known his name, but Bob didn't mind.

Mr. Tambourine Man
THE BYRDS

LOU RE

Johnny Cash
It ain't me babe

ETER, PAUL & M
owin' In The

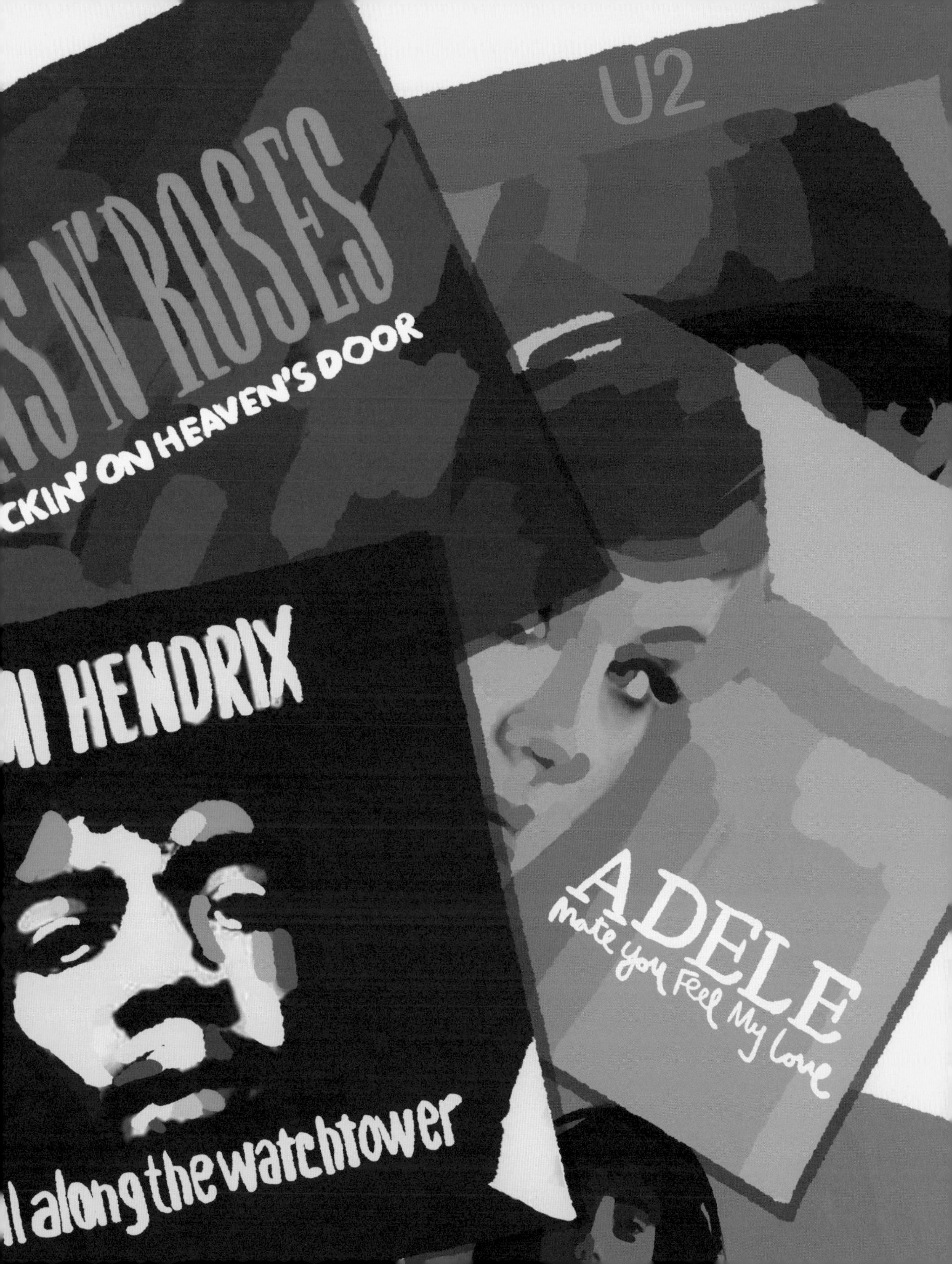
U2
S N' ROSES
CKIN' ON HEAVEN'S DOOR
MI HENDRIX
ll along the watchtower
ADELE
make you Feel My love

Instead of giving interviews or playing at being a star, Bob preferred to keep to himself. For him, a perfect day was working on a poem, riding around on his motorcycle, or talking with friends.

Being an artist meant being free and not caring about what others might think. Bob moved from folk to rock or pop, trying new sounds and exploring different styles, challenging himself as well as his fans.

He received all the awards an artist could dream of. And he was the first musician ever to be recognized with a Nobel Prize for Literature. But—in true Bob style—he didn't show up to the ceremony.

Today, little Bob—one of the greatest musicians and poets of all time—feels cool just being himself. He's an ordinary person who says what he thinks and does what he likes most: writing songs.

BOB DYLAN

(Born 1941)

1961   1966

Born Robert Allen Zimmerman, Bob grew up with his little brother
and parents, Abram and Beatrice. Bob's grandparents emigrated
from Russia to the United States in 1905, and the family soon
became part of a close-knit Jewish community of Hibbing,
Minnesota. Bob's father, Abram, owned an electrical appliance shop,
and there Bob first listened to blues and country music stations, and
later, rock and roll. After several performances in the high school
band, Bob went to the University of Minneapolis, where he changed
his name and started to make folk music, which had "more feeling
than rock and roll." He soon dropped out of college and moved to
New York, where he met the famous Woody Guthrie and quickly

1975   2012

became his disciple. Befriending a community of folk musicians and supporting artists such as John Lee Hooker at shows, Bob soon became one of America's most promising young talents. Known not just for his performances, he was brilliant at writing songs that expressed what people felt and thought. He signed his first record deal at age 20 with Columbia Records, and quickly became known as one of the most original and poetic voices in popular music. Bob went on to win multiple awards for his contribution to music and literature, but his greatest achievement was simply "being himself." At a time of great change, Bob's music gave people a voice, and his work continues to do so for millions of listeners, young and old, today.

Want to find out more about **Bob Dylan?**

Read this great book:

Forever Young by Bob Dylan and Paul Rogers

Brimming with creative inspiration, how-to projects, and useful information to enrich your everyday life, Quarto Knows is a favorite destination for those pursuing their interests and passions. Visit our site and dig deeper with our books into your area of interest: Quarto Creates, Quarto Cooks, Quarto Homes, Quarto Lives, Quarto Drives, Quarto Explores, Quarto Gifts, or Quarto Kids.

Text copyright © 2020 Maria Isabel Sánchez Vegara. Illustrations copyright © 2020 Conrad Roset.

Original concept of the series by Maria Isabel Sánchez Vegara, published by Alba Editorial, s.l.u

Produced under trademark licence from Alba Editorial s.l.u and Beautifool Couple S.L.

First Published in the US in 2020 by Frances Lincoln Children's Books, an imprint of The Quarto Group.

100 Cummings Center, Suite 265D, Beverly, MA 01915, USA.

T +1 978-282-9590 F +1 078-283-2742 **www.QuartoKnows.com**

First Published in Spain in 2020 under the title Pequeño & Grande Bob Dylan

by Alba Editorial, s.l.u., Baixada de Sant Miquel, 1, 08002 Barcelona

www.albaeditorial.es

All rights reserved.

Published by arrangement with Alba Editorial, s.l.u. Translation rights arranged by IMC Agència Literària, SL

All rights reserved.

A catalog record for this book is available from the British Library.

ISBN 978-0-7112-4675-1

eISBN 978-0-7112-5502-9

Set in Futura BT.

Published by Katy Flint • Designed by Karissa Santos

Edited by Rachel Williams • Production by Caragh McAleenan

Manufactured in Guangdong, China CC122020

9 7 5 4 6 8

Photographic acknowledgments (pages 28–29, from left to right) 1. Bob Dylan recording, 1961 © Michael Ochs Archives via Getty. 2. Bob Dylan, 1966 © Hulton Archive via Getty Images 3. Singer/Songwriter Bob Dylan performs, 1975 © Michael Ochs Archives via Getty. 4. US President Barack Obama presents the US Presidential Presidential Medal of Freedom to musician Bob Dylan during a ceremony on May 29, 2012 in the East Room of the White House in Washington , 2012 © AFP via Getty.

Collect the Little People, BIG DREAMS™ series:

FRIDA KAHLO

ISBN: 978-1-84780-783-0

COCO CHANEL

ISBN: 978-1-84780-784-7

MAYA ANGELOU

ISBN: 978-1-84780-889-9

AMELIA EARHART

ISBN: 978-1-84780-888-2

AGATHA CHRISTIE

ISBN: 978-1-84780-960-5

MARIE CURIE

ISBN: 978-1-84780-962-9

ROSA PARKS

ISBN: 978-1-78603-018-4

AUDREY HEPBURN

ISBN: 978-1-78603-053-5

EMMELINE PANKHURST

ISBN: 978-1-78603-020-7

ELLA FITZGERALD

ISBN: 978-1-78603-087-0

ADA LOVELACE

ISBN: 978-1-78603-076-4

JANE AUSTEN

ISBN: 978-1-78603-120-4

GEORGIA O'KEEFFE

ISBN: 978-1-78603-122-8

HARRIET TUBMAN

ISBN: 978-1-78603-227-0

ANNE FRANK

ISBN: 978-1-78603-229-4

MOTHER TERESA

ISBN: 978-1-78603-230-0

JOSEPHINE BAKER

ISBN: 978-1-78603-228-7

L. M. MONTGOMERY

ISBN: 978-1-78603-233-1

JANE GOODALL

ISBN: 978-1-78603-231-7

SIMONE DE BEAUVOIR

ISBN: 978-1-78603-232-4

MUHAMMAD ALI

ISBN: 978-1-78603-331-4

STEPHEN HAWKING

ISBN: 978-1-78603-333-8

MARIA MONTESSORI

ISBN: 978-1-78603-755-8

VIVIENNE WESTWOOD

ISBN: 978-1-78603-757-2

MAHATMA GANDHI

ISBN: 978-1-78603-787-9

DAVID BOWIE

ISBN: 978-1-78603-332-1

WILMA RUDOLPH

ISBN: 978-1-78603-751-0

DOLLY PARTON

ISBN: 978-1-78603-760-2

BRUCE LEE

ISBN: 978-1-78603-789-3

RUDOLF NUREYEV

ISBN: 978-1-78603-791-6

ZAHA HADID

ISBN: 978-1-78603-745-9

MARY SHELLEY

ISBN: 978-1-78603-748-0

MARTIN LUTHER KING JR.

ISBN: 978-0-7112-4567-9

DAVID ATTENBOROUGH

ISBN: 978-0-7112-4564-8

ASTRID LINDGREN

ISBN: 978-0-7112-5217-2

EVONNE GOOLAGONG

ISBN: 978-0-7112-4586-0

BOB DYLAN

ISBN: 978-0-7112-4675-1

ALAN TURING

ISBN: 978-0-7112-4678-2

BILLIE JEAN KING

ISBN: 978-0-7112-4693-5

GRETA THUNBERG

ISBN: 978-0-7112-5645-3

JESSE OWENS
ISBN: 978-0-7112-4583-9

JEAN-MICHEL BASQUIAT
ISBN: 978-0-7112-4580-8

ARETHA FRANKLIN

ISBN: 978-0-7112-4686-7

CORAZON AQUINO

ISBN: 978-0-7112-4684-3

PELÉ

ISBN: 978-0-7112-4573-0

ERNEST SHACKLETON

ISBN: 978-0-7112-4571-6

STEVE JOBS

ISBN: 978-0-7112-4577-8

AYRTON SENNA
ISBN: 978-0-7112-4672-0

LOUISE BOURGEOIS

ISBN: 978-0-7112-4690-4

ELTON JOHN

ISBN: 978-0-7112-5840-2

JOHN LENNON

ISBN: 978-0-7112-5767-2

PRINCE

ISBN: 978-0-7112-5439-8

CHARLES DARWIN

ISBN: 978-0-7112-5771-9

CAPTAIN TOM MOORE
ISBN: 978-0-7112-6209-6

HANS CHRISTIAN ANDERSEN

ISBN: 978-0-7112-5934-8

STEVIE WONDER

ISBN: 978-0-7112-5775-7

MEGAN RAPINOE

ISBN: 978-0-7112-5783-2

MARY ANNING

ISBN: 978-0-7112-5554-8

MALALA YOUSAFZAI

ISBN: 978-0-7112-5904-1

ACTIVITY BOOKS

STICKER ACTIVITY BOOK

ISBN: 978-0-7112-6012-2

COLORING BOOK

ISBN: 978-0-7112-6136-5

LITTLE ME, BIG DREAMS JOURNAL

ISBN: 978-0-7112-4889-2

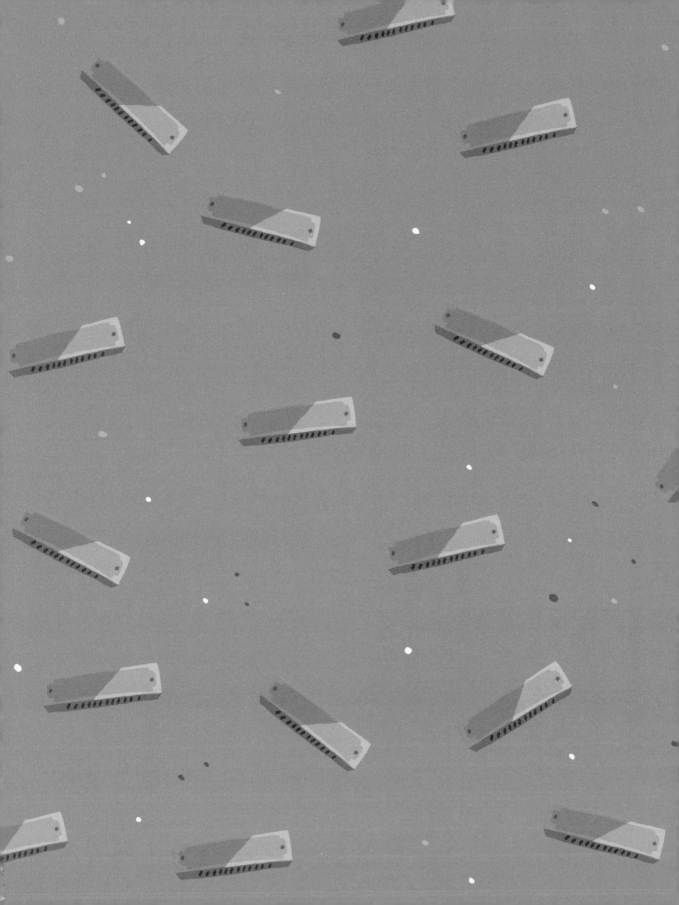